SO-CPE-941

Taylor's Secret

by Mary Frances Golson
Illustrated by Nicole Tadgell

Taylor slowly stirred his oatmeal. His mother was reading the newspaper.

"Mom," said Taylor, "today's the class trip."

"Yes, I know," said Mom.

"I can't go. It may rain, and I forgot where I put my raincoat."

Mom said, "The paper says it'll be sunny today."

"I think I lost the permission slip."

Mom said, "I put it in your backpack."

"I have a stomachache, and I may throw up."

Mom lowered the paper to look at Taylor.

"Why don't you want to go on the class trip? What's the *real* reason?"

Taylor couldn't look at her. He mumbled, "It's a stupid trip."

"Taylor Lee Gaines, stop acting like a preschooler. The trip is prepaid, and you're going."

After lunch Taylor and his classmates arrived
at the nonprofit Needles Nature Center where a
volunteer greeted them.

"I'll be showing you some of our animals,"
Joan explained. "People bring us sick or injured
wild animals, and we try to heal them. If we can,
we'll release them back into the wild. If we can't,
they'll stay here with us."

Joan stopped next to a cage.

"This beaver had a mishap with a trail bike," she said. "See its oversized front teeth? It uses them to cut down trees. Beavers are amazing builders."

The other children moved in closer. Taylor remained at the back. He wouldn't admit it, but he was a little afraid of wild animals.

Joan turned to the next cage.

"This hawk was struck by an arrow," she said. "See its keen eyes? It's a good hunter. From high in the sky it can spot a small rabbit far below in a meadow."

The hawk suddenly flapped its wings. Taylor could imagine the hawk sailing high overhead. He moved a little closer.

Joan walked to another cage.

"This owl got its feet cut by some wire," she said. "Like the hawk, it's a good hunter, but it hunts at night. It can see as well at midnight as the hawk can see at noon."

The owl's huge yellow eyes seemed to look straight at Taylor. He moved closer.

At home Taylor talked nonstop about the animals he'd seen. His mother was surprised and pleased. She knew about Taylor's fear.

"I'm glad you had such a good time," she said. "Maybe next weekend we can go to the zoo."

Taylor didn't answer. He was busy drawing a picture of a hawk gliding high in the sky.